I'm cute - and God I hate that. Because that's not cool. I'm like your niece, and nobody wants to date their niece. It's the chubby cheeks. The whole reason people voted for me on American Idol is because I'm an everyday, normal girl.

Kelly Clarkson

Because you have things like 'American Idol' and you've got radio stations that play music made entirely by computers, it's easy to forget there are bands with actual people playing actual instruments that rock.

Dave Grohl

Since we launched the original 'Pop Idol' in England, I've remained close with Simon Fuller. Working as executive producer on 'American idol' for its first seven years not only was an inspirational journey into the heart of American pop culture, it opened my eyes to the untapped potential of the incredibly dynamic young people in this world.

Nigel Lythgoe

This is a frightening statistic. More people vote in 'American Idol' than in any US election.

Rush Limbaugh

Who's judging American Idol? Paula Abdul? Paula Abdul judging a singing contest is like Christopher Reeve judging a dance contest!

Chris Rock

We aren't handicapped in any way except by what other people think. Focus on people's abilities. I can't be on 'American Idol,' but there's all kinds of stuff I can do.

Marlee Matlin

Americans have been dumbed down to the point where more people watching 'American Idol' than listen to the state of the union address. And that's too bad. I'm not trying to take any bread out of the mouth of Simon Cowell, but if the president is speaking to the people of the United States, and people are going to watch 'American Idol,' that's sad.

Henry Rollins

I don't watch 'American Idol.' I don't watch any of that stuff.

Denis Leary

Instead of plotting the demise of the traditional family, as some politicians and religious leaders would have you believe, gay people mow their lawns and watch 'American Idol' and video their children's concerts and have the same hopes and dreams that their straight counterparts do.

Jodi Picoult

I've never bought a Dylan record. A singing poet? It just bores me to tears. I've got to tell you, if I had 10 Dylans in the final of 'American Idol,' we would not be getting 30 million viewers a week. I don't believe the Bob Dylans of this world would make 'American Idol 'a better show.

Simon Cowell

The biggest risk I've ever taken is going on American Idol and trying to be myself. I wasn't going to try too hard to conform, and I knew that it could possibly not work out.

Adam Lambert

Don't go on American Idol, I think you'll spend the rest of your life living it down and I think it's getting kinda scary, isn't it?

Joe Cocker

The 'American Idol' and 'X Factor' shows, they're great shows. But I think I need to make a show like that, directed straight to the hood, to the artists that don't get the attention, that don't have the money to make themselves representable.

Snoop Dogg

I look up to my brother - he inspires me so much. He has always been my best friend. He knows everything. I left the house at 16 when I auditioned for 'American Idol' and he was 14. It was one of those things that was so sudden and neither of us expected it. He has been so supportive of me even though I know that every time I leave, it hurts him.

Jordin Sparks

I've told many people that I'm not looking to go out there and find the most beautiful girl in the world who likes me because I'm 'Mr. American Idol Scott McCreery.' If I could just find a nice hometown girl who just likes me for who I am, that's all I want.

Scotty McCreery

A lot of the new people they choose on shows like 'American Idol' and things like that - I don't ever hear lead singers. They always seem to choose to pick people that are great singers, fabulous singers, but they've never got the voice that makes a great lead singer.

Roger Daltrey

If you don't have any ties to the music industry, you just love 'American Idol,' you can sit there and do exactly what you do in your living room, which is stare at them and judge them.

Neil Patrick Harris

I'm not trying to be evasive, but when I say yes and no, I say 'yes' because there are narrow-minded people that won't look past the logo and 'no' because 'American Idol' put me in front of millions of people and I would not have a career without 'Idol.'

Bo Bice

I would lose straight away if I went on 'American Idol.'

Tom DeLonge

Long before 'American Idol', people used to call me a diva. And I be like, 'Hold on, are you calling me something else on the sly? You gonna call me a diva, call me a good diva.'

Jennifer Hudson

'American Idol' is sometimes lumped with reality shows and it has that element - folks-next-door battling it out in a contest. But instead of fighting leeches, bugs, parasites and each other, as on CBS's 'Survivor' and other shows that imitate it, the 'American Idol' contestants, of course, sing.

Tom Shales

I don't want to be the cliche American Idol dude. I want to be different, you know - that's the whole goal, me and music. It's about being yourself and being unique.

Paul McDonald

I want to figure out what kind of artist I want to be, because with the 'American Idol' process, it just works really fast. The night of the finale, they said, 'OK, here are all the label people that you're gonna work with, this is the album you're gonna make and blah, blah, blah.' So it was a pretty fast process, but it's been cool.

David Archuleta

If we had to choose one American Idol to go out to dinner with, it would be Fantasia. There are no airs and graces about her... I like her.

Simon Cowell

There's a lot of things that are said on the American Idol message board. I quit reading them because most of the people are very mean.

Carrie Underwood

American Idol transcends age, gender, ethnicity, everything.

Carrie Underwood

The TV is often on in our house, but I really only keep up with three shows: 'American Idol,' 'Modern Family' and 'The Walking Dead.' Sometimes I'll sip red wine - it's a nice way to slow down and relax.

Carrie Underwood

I think one of the things I was shocked about was how interested the world is in 'American Idol' and how people, writers, they write about 'Idol' all the time, and I guess I didn't expect that.

Nicki Minaj

American Idol allowed us to find Carrie Underwood.

Luke Bryan

The whole 'American Idol' way of looking at things is the antithesis of what I grew up with. There are a whole lot of kids wanting to be famous now, whereas if I'd even mentioned that word to one of my teachers, I would have got into a whole load of trouble.

Harry Connick, Jr.

I've never seen American Idol but I am grateful to them. That show is one of Fox's biggest moneymakers, and some of that

money goes to pay for shows like Prison Break. Simon
Cowell's been signing my paychecks and for that I say thanks.

Wentworth Miller

Look at 'American Idol,' which I don't look at. Those winners
haven't become household names except for Jennifer Hudson,
and she was a reject. You can't aim to be a household name.
You just have to be successful.

Andre Leon Talley

I'm excited about the new judges on 'American Idol.' Jennifer
Lopez was a real mentor to me my season and I admire her so
much. And I kind of have a crush on Steven Tyler. It's going to
be interesting to see is one person going to stand out among
the judges or if everyone will sort of be equal.

Jordin Sparks

I wouldn't have made it past the first round of American Idol
auditions. It was months before our first song was recorded.
The guys were like, 'Just seeng!' And I was like, 'I don't know
how to seeng! Can't I just play the triangle?'

Malin Akerman

Just the title of 'American Idol' is something that people can
look up to. I'm not Saint Scott, I'm not Mr. Perfect, but I want
to be that role model.

Scotty McCreery

There are plenty of people who are willing to pay $2.6 million for 30 seconds on the Super Bowl and hundreds of thousands of dollars for 'American Idol.' There will be advertising dollars on the Internet. We're there as well. We win either way.

Leslie Moonves

You know, when I did 'American Idol' the three times, I tried to tell these kids you have to tell the story of the lyric.

Barry Manilow

American Idol' is a $900 million-a-year corporation. When you are dealing with that, you can't come off with lies - it's either the truth or nothing.

Corey Clark

I am broadcaster's biggest cheerleader because I genuinely believe in it. Where else can you get 20 million people a week watching 'NCIS' or 'American Idol?' Where else can you get 120 million watching the Super Bowl?

Leslie Moonves

I will always appreciate 'American Idol,' and I never forget about where I come from.

Lee DeWyze

These days, with 'American Idol' and all the other reality shows, young people become famous overnight, and that can be very difficult to handle, the way photographers follow you around and study your every move.

Barry Manilow

The people that go on 'American Idol' do want some recognition and fame.

Kimberly Caldwell

Well, being that, at the house and being in the competition, it was very hard to be with family. We couldn't have visitors out of respect for everyone else there. But, being the American Idol, the focus would have been on me.

LaToya London

I have a bit of a problem with 'American Idol.' Forgive me, but it's difficult for me to watch. I can't help but think of people being exploited. On the other hand, I'm really enjoying 'Glee.'

Lesley Gore

In all honesty, I'm not able to talk about contracts. It's nothing with 'American Idol' in particular, it's just things I really need to take care of in my life.

Mario Vazquez

'American Idol' has done a great job of defaming my name and throwing a lot of mud at me for the past two years, so that set up a lot of roadblocks for me.

Corey Clark

At the end of the day, it is about the album and book and also about setting the record straight, because 'American Idol' has done a great job of defaming my name and throwing a lot of mud at me for the past two years. So that set up a lot of roadblocks for me.

Corey Clark

I was very honored to get to be part of 'American Idol.'

Dolly Parton

I've never watched an entire episode of 'American Idol'. It's too mean.

Christina Aguilera

I created 'America's Next Top Model' one-hundred percent. I was in my kitchen making tea one morning, and I looked out the window, and the idea popped into my head. I wanted it to be 'American Idol' meets 'Ford Supermodel of the Year' meets 'The Real World.'

Tyra Banks

I don't watch 'American Idol,' but I wouldn't call it 'undignified.'

Buzz Aldrin

I think after coming off of 'American Idol'... people kind of expect you to just be awesome all the time, and we're still learning. I had a lot of stage experience, but it was in a 200-seat theater, you know - it wasn't thousands of people in front of me.

Carrie Underwood

'American Idol' has taken over my whole life.

Paula Abdul

I think the attraction of 'American Idol' is about the basic human nature attitude that is, 'We can put you up there. But we can take you down.'

Quincy Jones

I watch 'The Voice' and 'American Idol,' and I sit in my Brookstone foot massager. It's so exciting at my house.

Jennifer Love Hewitt

I've been watching 'American Idol' since its debut season in 2002. Back then, America hadn't yet evolved into a gladiatorial cybernation of bloggers, tweeters, and self-ordained voice coaches.

Diablo Cody

I was on TV for almost sixteen weeks during American Idol. It's at the point now where it's old.

Clay Aiken

'American Idol' has changed the face of television.

Jennifer Hudson

I enjoy watching Fear Factor, Newlyweds and American Idol as far as reality TV shows go.

Natalie Gulbis

American Idol, I love. I think it's a passing fancy but not passing so soon.

Diane Sawyer

I'm also a big 'American Idol' fan. I think it's just great fun.

Jim Parsons

I'm a big 'American Idol' watcher, and sometimes I like to watch 'America's Got Talent.' Those are big, corny admissions, but sometimes it's so fun to see those kids really sing their hearts out.

Katey Sagal

I definitely wanted to be an actor. I didn't want to be on TV, I didn't want to be famous, I didn't want to be anyone in particular; I just wanted to do it. I see young people now who look at magazines, or American Idol and their goal is to have that lifestyle - to have good handbags, or go out with cute guys from shows, or whatever. But I definitely wanted to be an actor.

Lauren Graham

I was always in bands before, but on 'American Idol,' it was about getting my voice out there. It was always my goal, though, to get a band together again.

Chris Daughtry

'American Idol' became a juggernaut of epic proportions, but to me it was always like home.

Nigel Lythgoe

Hip-hop is a way of life. It isn't a genre in truth in 'American Idol.'

Nigel Lythgoe

Obviously neither 'American Idol' nor 'Dancing With the Stars' is a variety show in the classic sense, but the way they incorporate elements of drama, comedy and suspense is moderately ingenious.

Tom Shales

Most people use Twitter to meet girls, and I use it to meet 'American Idol' contestants!

Chris Jericho

I auditioned for 'American Idol' at 17. They told me, 'No.'

Amber Riley

I doubt the terrorists saw 9/11 as a teaching opportunity. And we're not really a culture geared to anything as humble as 'learning.' But I was disappointed in how quickly everyone wanted to get back to normal. It was as if we watched terrorism on TV for a while, then got bored and turned back to 'American Idol.'

Jess Walter

Have you seen 'American Idol' lately? I'm sure that some kids somewhere at this moment are thrashing themselves silly over what they call 'Rock n' Roll.'

Eric Burdon

I knew people liked me on 'American Idol,' but I didn't think they'd care to come see me sing at my own show.

David Archuleta

An American Idol is someone that has all the qualities that America thinks is positive, attractive and alluring.

Mario Vazquez

Some people choose to go on 'American Idol' or another singing contest, and some people choose to beat down barrooms before anyone even knows who they are, in order to get a fan base, so when they do get a record deal, they have that to put in front of a label.

Jake Owen

I don't think rap really fits in to 'American Idol' in the sense that I believe rap is an art form in itself more akin to poetry, more akin to drama, if you will.

Nigel Lythgoe

Winning 'American Idol' is awesome.

Lee DeWyze

I think American Idol is a great career launcher. A blessing for all of us.

LaToya London

I love the 'Housewives.' I don't watch 'American Idol' or 'X Factor.' I guess I don't like network reality: I like my Bravo; I like documentary programming - I love 'Intervention' and some things on TLC more than others - but the 'Real Housewives' to me are really revolutionary, in terms of giving camera time to women of a certain age.

Julie Klausner

'American Idol' is the fast track to fame. I'm just lucky it worked out. I don't feel different. The way people react to me is different.

Crystal Bowersox

My weakness is 'American Idol.' My husband thinks it's ridiculous. But I am so inspired by those young people who are singing their guts out.

Mary Gordon

When I was younger, I definitely had more of a dream, as they say on 'American Idol,' that I would have my own show. I always thought that that was something that would happen, that eventually I would just get my own show because anyone who wants their own show should get their own show.

Scott Aukerman

Many movie stars or American Idol contestants sort of fall into theater... and say, 'Oh, yeah, I would love to do theater.' And then they get here and say, 'Oh, wait a minute, this actually is a craft!' It's not just show up one day and do it. It's show up eight times a week, twice on Wednesdays and twice on Saturdays.

Billy Porter

When one person does something that works, everyone else wants to do it. So it didn't surprise me at all to see people come with different versions of 'American Idol' and a lot of them are exactly the same but with different twists.

Ruben Studdard

I've been wanting to sing for a long time. I've been singing all my life, and I've tried different record companies, but it seemed like - it was such a struggle and so hard to get out there. So, I said, 'I'm gonna go on American Idol and see how far it takes me.'

Fantasia Barrino

I do watch 'American Idol' sometimes. It's not really that pleasurable... I take that back. It is the epitome of a guilty pleasure. Sometimes there's some good singers on that show.

M. Ward

Before 'American Idol' and all this stuff, I was obsessed with music charts, and I used to go online to find out what was popular in other countries. I'd log on to the BBC website, and that's how I found out about artists like Natasha Bedingfield, Daniel Bedingfield and Take That.

David Archuleta

Especially now, with 'Glee,' it's allowed a lot of kids to love music and performing at a young age. All ages watched

'American Idol,' but I think it was nice to be able to show kids, 'Hey, you can be here, too.'

David Archuleta

Who wouldn't want to be an 'American Idol' judge? It's an awesome, awesome show.

Jane Krakowski

I think a big part of 'American Idol' that scares people and actually has, I'm sure, stopped people from trying out is the fact that you do have to do things that are necessarily not your genre.

Lee DeWyze

If I have a name out there from this thing called 'American Idol,' I don't understand why anyone wouldn't use it for good. That's the way the world should work.

Crystal Bowersox

It's not a natural process, 'American Idol,' but it does great things for the people that are on that show. If you don't walk away from it with some kind of positive outlook or find an opportunity to come from it, then I feel like that's a choice.

Crystal Bowersox

Frankly, if 'American Idol' was the way I'd have to audition as a singer, I'd be standing behind the counter in a 5&10 right now. I couldn't have done it that way.

Lesley Gore

An American Idol is someone who knows how to change people's lives through music.

Anwar Robinson

I think America did a great job. I think Carrie Underwood fits the bill of American Idol. She's a wonderful girl, and she's gonna have a great career.

Bo Bice

My favorite type of music to sing and to listen to, you know, rock. It's not always metal, but you know, half the time it is. Metal's cool, you know? Not everybody on 'American Idol' listens to metal.

James Durbin

If millions of Americans choose to weigh in on the outcome of 'American Idol' through text messages and the Web, then why not harness similar technological tools to encourage discourse on the political landscape?

Ruzwana Bashir

I got to play with ZZ Top and introduce Bryan Adams and George Michael. And to have it all topped off by me winning 'American Idol?!' It's pretty absurd.

David Cook

I've tried to move on with my life and my career for the last two years and do my own thing, and 'American Idol' and FOX, they've just been making it really tough for me to do that.

Corey Clark

The landscape is television has changed so much, because there are so many outlets, that the odds of getting a zeitgeisty hit - you know how 'American Idol' seems to appeal to every human being on the planet? Doing that in comedy nowadays is very, very hard.

Bill Lawrence

I definitely love 'Camelot.' It's my favorite show. I'm a big 'True Blood' fan. I love 'American Idol,' and I love my girl J-Lo. The rest are my homework shows: 'Forensic Files,' 'Dr. G. Medical Examiner,' 'The First 48.'

Tamala Jones

At the time, the only options were playing the local county fair. Now with American Idol and younger recording artists that have come out, there is more of an opportunity.

Marla Sokoloff

It was a pleasure to work with everybody at 'American Idol' and to be able to be part of the 'Idol' family.

Katie Stevens